A FEW HOURS OF SMART WORK

OR

A LIFETIME OF HARD WORK?

SWAPNA GOPINATH

Envision Earth Media

First published in paperback in 2020
By Envision Earth Media
A division of The Open Circle LLC, USA

Price: US $4.49
ISBN # 9781733083836

Envision Earth Media,
A division of The Open Circle LLC,
902 Gribbin Ln 3B,
Toledo OH 43612,
USA.
www.envisionearthmedia.com

"The Law of Attraction requires regular practice to ensure extraordinary results. This book is a valuable and easy-to-read guide to manifest whatever you want in life. Even busy people can effectively use the simple methods described by the writer, in their daily life."
-   **Prabhath P, Editor-in-Chief & Chief Operations Officer, Envision Earth Media**

"This book has the power to change your life for the better. The science and psychology of it are simple to grasp. Through daily habits, one is able to rewire the subconscious mind to always be on course to fulfill our deepest desire."
-   **Amy I. Ramdass, Chief Creative Coordinator, Envision Earth Media**

CONTENTS

ABOUT THE AUTHOR

Swapna Gopinath was born in the Kerala state of India, renowned as 'God's Own Country,' and was raised in another equally beautiful place near the sea, Goa. Armed with a Masters in Business Administration and a passion for numbers, she was a part of the talent acquisition function for various multinationals for over 12 years. Currently, she is the Chief Marketing and Promotions Manager of Envision Earth Media and Envision Earth Magazine. Swapna grew up with an ardent interest in reading. She has now ventured into writing. In her spare time, she enjoys travelling, reading and trying different cuisines worldwide.

This book, on the subject of the Law of Attraction, is her second spiritual book, detailing her own daily routine and methods that have worked for her in the process of manifesting her dream life. Her first Kindle E-book *Cherry Picking for the Lazy Bums* entered the Amazon bestseller list by reaching the highest rank of #79 on amazon.com and #6 on amazon.ca. It presents practical and simplified methods related to the Law of Attraction that as many people as possible can practise to enrich their lives, and is based on her extensive research on the Law of Attraction besides the real-life miracles she has experienced.

Email: swapna7774@gmail.com

Facebook: www.facebook.com/AuthorSwapnaGopinath

FOREWORD

When I was invited to write this foreword, I only knew a little about Swapna from a friend of mine who had told me. But I have always had an interest in the Law of Attraction and how we can create the reality and life we desire and deserve as human beings. So of course, I was interested. As the CEO of a conscious media company and publisher of an upcoming spiritual magazine, I love to see powerful ideas presented in a simple and relatable way that doesn't dilute the message or principles, and Swapna's book does exactly that.

Too often, manifesting what we want in our daily life, let alone living our dreams, just seems too hard or too much work. But Swapna shows how to effortlessly begin shifting your mind-set and perspective to abundance and the acceptance of your dreams as something you can make real and tangible, by using the power of gratitude. Thank you for sharing this wonderful book! There is so much power in that simple statement "Thank you." It opens you up and prepares you to start using the wonderful techniques explained in this book for which you only need a few minutes a day to change the rest of your life!

One of the beautiful things about this book is that it is a simple step-by-step way of incorporating the LOA into your daily life. Theories abound on how the LOA works, but not every book or video gives you a simple yet profound way to quickly integrate it into your life. Swapna doesn't just give you a great way to make the Law of Attraction a part of your life, she also gives you the same methods she used herself that have worked for her and are still working for her, and many others every day! You will even discover how to use water to help you achieve your dreams!

So prepare yourself to begin living your dreams!

Warm Regards,

Alex N. Moyer,
Chief Executive Officer,
Envision Earth Media
www.envisionearthmedia.com

PREFACE

The Law of Attraction can often be a little overwhelming, especially if you are a novice at practising it. However, don't despair. If you attempt to put in a fair bit of regular practice, you will begin to see miracles unfold in your life too.

This book specifies what has worked for me. Endless methods and practices show up when it comes to your urge to manifest according to the Law of Attraction. Some prefer certain methods that work in their favour and do away with the ones that do not yield them positive results. And I am not surprised if there are others for whom no method works. Faith and belief in your own ability to attract the life of your choice has to be of primary importance, without which none of the methods would ever be effective.

I have personally experienced an endless list of miracles most often, if not every day, and my life has indeed become magnificent.

This book highlights the practices that I follow and is focussed on a one-day schedule of my life. Initially, I too had my share of doubts which was gradually erased with each desire shaping to fulfilment. Now there isn't a single thing on planet Earth that can deter me from practising these methods on a daily basis.

I would recommend these simplified practices so that others too can follow suit. I am absolutely convinced that nothing is impossible if you put your mind to it! Try it … to experience it.

Love,
Swapna Gopinath

ACKNOWLEDGMENTS

This is a book that has special significance in my life. And as usual, I enjoyed penning down every word.

I am thankful to each and every person who has contributed to the successful completion of this book.

I am immensely grateful to Mr. Prabhath P, who tirelessly put in an effort to work closely on this project by providing comprehensive help in the editing area. I thank him for his invaluable editorial assistance and endorsement comment.

My heartfelt thanks to Mr. Alex N. Moyer for penning a foreword for this book amidst his busy schedule and publishing it through Envision Earth Media.

My sincere gratitude to Ms. Amy Ramdass for converting the book manuscript in a professional manner to Kindle, PDF E-book and print formats, and also for uploading the book to the Amazon platform properly. I am grateful to her for endorsing the book too.

A special 'Thank you' to my dear friends Sushmita and Preety who have served as my support system all through the writing of my books.

My never-ending thanks to my parents. My dad is no more but he has been truly my inspiration throughout my life's journey. My darling mom is the pillar of my strength. Her intense faith in me is incredible. Thank you.

I want to thank the sunshine of my life, Nihal Nadayil, who is my heartbeat in the literal sense, for his consistent inspiration and endless encouragement. He has taught me to live all my dreams.

I thank God for every miracle that has happened and continues to happen in my life. I am eternally grateful for his divine guidance to deliver the book in the best possible way that I can conceive of.

1. CREATE YOUR DREAM LIFE

You are the creator of your life. You are the architect of your life. The canvas of your life is in your hands, so paint it the way you want. Give it your best as the colours you splurge on your canvas is what you get to see in reality.

You are the superhero of your own movie called 'My life.' Act the role the way you want it. Play it to perfection. Your movie is in your mind and your mind creates your reality. The remote control of your reality is in your palm.

I am living my 'Dream Life.' Are you too living the life you wished for? I love my life and I am living it to the fullest. I have full control of my life because I know with utmost certainty that I create my destiny.

I believe that each one of us should lead our dream life without any financial worries and with an overflowing bank account that is stocked with cash. You should be able to travel to different countries, wear designer clothes, taste the exquisite cuisines from all over the world, dine at the finest restaurants, stay in any of the five and seven-star hotels in the world, own fancy cars, live in luxurious homes and be surrounded with people who love and care for you, while your life is filled with endless happiness, laughter and immense fun.

1

Imagine your life if you could spend money without counting. Oh! La La. What a life!! It is truly magical. We can CREATE our lives exactly the way we want it to be and the beauty of it all is that you are the creator of your beautiful life. Get your best intentions in the open so that you can make your life absolutely colourful.

Let me begin by leading you through the few practices that truly work for me in any circumstances. I have exponentially benefitted from my practice of the LOA and experienced my life scale up several notches, all because of a few hours of deliberate smart work.

2. ESTABLISH A MORNING ROUTINE

I spring up from bed every day, charged to live my intentionally designed life. It's absolutely dream-like. Wouldn't you too want to be the designer of your own life? Wouldn't you want to design your life to your taste?

There are so many people who begin their day by turning off the alarm and going back to sleep. The end result is that they eventually get late for work and get stressed out in the attempt to reach the workplace on time. Some of them are habituated to waking up to sad songs or loud eardrum-cracking music, the first thing in the morning. Some others drag themselves out of bed, practically cursing and hating the first few hours of the day, especially if it happens to be a Saturday in the Arab world and a Monday for the rest of the world. Yes, I know a lot of people who suffer from Saturday blues and Monday blues!

People are rushing for work amidst the hustle and bustle of the traffic, and the work pressure only adds to the already existing high blood pressure, for some of them. For certain others, the boss is a pain, the job sucks, the paycheque fails to make the ends meet, and there is also another lot of people who literally hate their own lives. Do you relate to any of these?

3

If so, let us work to turn our world around and make it the magical world we would like it to be. Let's make it the fairy tale world we would love to live in. Let's aim to design it to be the ultimate luxurious life so that we no longer aspire for anything that money cannot buy. Let's work and create our lives to be truly magical, in every possible way.

Many of you are plain lazy. Such people are likely to find endless excuses for being unable to spend 15 minutes to half an hour, on a daily basis, to practise the Law of Attraction that has the potential to change your life forever.

What if I told you that you have the power to change your life to the extent that you need not work in a job that makes you unhappy, you need not work tirelessly for small paycheques or for a paltry amount that is not sufficient to meet your daily needs, you need not wake up early and crib about going to work? Instead, you could choose what you wish to do with your life and you have the ability to make it absolutely magnificent.

You can stay in a beautiful house, own the best car, have the perfect relationship, travel the world, be famous and live all your dreams. Yes, you can do all of this by just sparing a few precious minutes of your life every day for some basic activities that have the potential to change your life drastically. So pull yourself up and grant the journey of your life the precious half an hour every day unfailingly, in order to change your life and move the pendulum from being unhappy to living blissfully. Stop wondering why you are alive in the first place ... The fact that you are alive itself is a blessing!

The most important thing is to begin to think positive thoughts. There are a lot of people who are constantly in a negative state of mind. They are perpetually sad, unhappy, seeking revenge, jealous, hurt, crying, depressed, hyper-sensitive, misunderstood and greedy. In fact, some of them are quite contented being negative and keep harbouring such regressive thoughts. Often people who have this kind of a mindset that is filled with negativity, do nothing about their lives.

They merely stand and watch their lives pass by like a spectator seated in a coffee shop who watches life elapse from a distance. They have seemingly accepted the passive role of a detached onlooker. How convenient is that? There is barely anything that they can do about their own lives. So this excuse that they are helpless and they can only contribute to their life by watching whatever is happening appears convenient. At times, deliberately choosing to be the helpless person in their own life

5

comes across as a relief to some because it gives them an alternative option to blame their predicament on fate. While some of them prefer the depressed lives they lead, they are fine with merely feeling sorry for themselves.

Do you truly wish to lead such a life? My advice to you is to let go of all negative thoughts and pessimistic attitudes towards your own life. You are the creator of your creation. Your creation, in this case, is your own life. You have the power to change your life and get whatever it is that you want, without a fragment of doubt. Then why would you choose to lead a life of unhappiness?

Don't wait until you hit rock-bottom, or end up depressed or wind up being a bitter person. You still have the time and resources to turn your world around to 180 degrees and usher it the way you want it. So let's begin to manoeuvre it in the direction of your choice.

If you can relate to what is stated above, change it. Change it now and stick to your everyday routine like glue. It's your magic wand, so use it to bring forth your desired life!

a) Start your day with gratitude

In today's time and age, when most of us wake up, the first thing we set our attention and eyes on, is our cell phone.

We are eager to know if there is an important message or any posts on Facebook or on any social media platform that may interest us. My suggestion to you is to kindly refrain from doing so.

When you wake up in the morning, you are known to be in the Vortex state. It means that your mind is at the most basic or natural condition. You have no resistance in this state of mind and your ability to manifest anything is at the peak. What more do you want? Put your plans into action and get going.

For your morning schedule, it is recommended that you wake up an hour earlier than the intended timing though you could still laze in bed, wrapped up cozily in your warm blanket, but there is an underlying compulsion to work on your thoughts. Set your mind into a positive thought frame.

You can do it by beginning your day, being grateful. You need to make it a practice to identify and be grateful for at least a handful of things you are genuinely happy for. They could be anything. Big or small, or anything about your family or your health or your physical attributes or wealth or pets or friends or your very ability to see, smell, taste, feel and hear. You name it.

The phrase 'Thank you' is so powerful. It raises your vibration and uplifts your energy. Every day, you come across people whose lives are wonderful and you also see people whose lives could be better. The ones whose lives have room for improvement have one thing in common. They lack gratitude for whatever they already have. Remember, no matter how bad your life or your current situation is, start saying the magical words 'Thank you.' You can never fail to realize your life turning 360 degrees, all for the better.

'Thank you' must be said for all the things around you, even for the things that are not going great in your life. You must say it even for the things you are anticipating. Expressing thanks puts you in the positive vibe of receiving much more pleasant things as the day unfolds. Ten minutes of nonstop feeling of gratitude clubbed with 'Thank you' certainly makes you feel so energised that it's already got you on to the momentum of being happy.

You need to be grateful for your past, your present and your awesome future. You need to be grateful and give thanks for whatever you already had in the past, whatever you currently have, and whatever you plan to manifest in the future as if it's already transpired in your life.

For example, if you plan to live in a bungalow in the future, you can begin to apply positive energy and gratitude by saying the following:

"I am so happy and grateful that I live in a four-bedroom house overlooking the sea. I am so happy and grateful that I have a magnificent view all around the house that is so soothing to my senses. I am so happy and grateful that my house represents peace and calm always. I am so happy and grateful, watching the happy expressions of my family members and friends who visit my house. Thank you, thank you, thank you, for the amazing house that I live in. I am truly grateful.

So use the golden words 'Thank you' as often as you can aloud or mentally. Whichever way, it creates wonders.

b) Set an intention deliberately for the day

After your ten minutes of being grateful and saying 'Thank you' for all that you can practically think of in your life, you can certainly move on to the next method of the Law of Attraction. You need to set an intention. Although 'intention' has never been much in the mainstream, it has a lot of potential to create wonders in your life.

You have to deliberately write down or verbally declare an

intention that can last all through the day. Some of you may tend to keep a gratitude book handy like I do. I jot down as well as voice it aloud several times a day. The intention here is directing your mind to achieve a particular goal.

"I intend to have a wonderful day filled with peace and happiness. People around me are in a fantastic mood and they lighten up the workplace with bright smiles!"

"I intend to have a relaxed day at work. The work is manageable and has a calming effect on me. I can work at my pace and at leisure."

"I intend to hear only positive and wonderful words all through the day. My boss is very encouraging and my colleagues are so cooperative and happy today!"

"I intend to be rich as soon as possible."

The above sentences are some of the examples which state your intention for the day or for an extended period of time. Always ensure that your intention comprises of positive words and statements. You might not have a soft spot for your boss or certain people at the office, but it doesn't affect you if you intend to be thankful for their outlook too as they indirectly impact you at the work front. I normally write down my intention and paste it on the wall opposite my bed.

It consists of two intentions. One focuses on a daily intention and another one is long-term! You too can do the same or declare it in your mind on a daily basis or say it aloud, whichever practice makes you comfortable.

Intention sets the tone for the day and as the day progresses, you will notice that your day is as pleasant as you asked for. In case, you have forgotten to practise intention in the morning, which is the appropriate time to set an intention for the day, then opt for doing it anytime within the first few hours of waking up. It is setting forth a clear desire about how you wish your day to progress.

Ask yourself how you want to feel throughout the day. Starting your day with an intention helps you to decide how your day must ideally unfold. So use your intention deliberately on a daily basis to make things work in your favour. It will surely change your life. And the beauty of it all is that it barely takes a couple of minutes and you are already set for the day with a positive outlook.

You are done with ten minutes of gratitude and five minutes of intention. So that makes it a total of 15 minutes of practising the LOA. Wow! You have set the ball rolling!

c) Do meditate for at least five minutes

As for the lazy lot, you can still continue to stay put in bed with the blanket all wrapped around you, but now you got to sit up. You must not lean or sit in a hunched manner. You can sit in any posture that makes you comfortable but do sit straight. That's a must. Your legs can be folded or you could adopt a lotus position or stretch your legs ahead of you. Your hands can be entwined into each other or stretched out on your sides on the bed or placed on your knees with the tips of your thumb and forefinger joined. Just be relaxed.

Concentrate between your eyebrows. Think of nothing. Am I asking for the absurd? Don't fret. Now the state of 'almost no thoughts' comes with practice ... Initially, it's obvious you are going to think of everything that is happening around you. You are bound to think of a million thoughts. Your mind is likely to wander in every possible direction. It might stray towards your choice of clothes that you plan to wear to work or the busy traffic on your way to the office or ponder on your supervisor's mood today or on your diet plans for the day or settle itself on last night's outing or stick to something that is bothering you lately, and so on. The list is endless. No problem. Don't pressure yourself. Let the thoughts come and go freely.

Gradually with time, you will reach a state where you are thinking

12

of nothing. You have reached a state of mind where you begin to see plain lines or blobs or colour. This is the appropriate time for you to put forth your desires and imagine them happening. Imagine the outcome, brimming with feeling. If it is a car you are wishing for, imagine everything about the car, overladen with feeling. You must feel like you own it already. It's right there in your parking. You are touching and feeling the glossy exterior. You are feeling the texture of its seat covers with your fingers. You can sense the smell of a brand-new car. Imagine the faces of your loved ones lighting up when you mention you are the proud owner of this car.

Dream about it as if it is for real … it's in your power ... nothing can stop you. The creation starts in your imagination. Hence, wherever your focus rests on, so does your energy. So take the bold step and imagine, dream and manifest everything you want!

3. DURING THE DAY ROUTINE

Develop the passion to change your life for the better. Do whatever it takes to make it a roaring success. You can put these practices into play as and when you have the time during the course of the day or on weekends. There are no shortcuts. You got to do it, at all costs.

a) Affirmations

Your morning regime is kind of complete and you can move on to other work-related activities. The lack of time applies to most of us but you must be smart enough to make the most of it.

I would recommend that you begin the first half of your day with affirmations. Affirmations are a wonderful method of manifesting whatever you desire. Do not give excuses like you are running short of time and therefore, couldn't put the Law of Attraction to practice. I can suggest several time slots where you can put affirmation into practice. You do have a lot of free time to think when you make coffee, wash the dishes, take a shower, wait for the signal to turn green on your way to work or shopping, wait for your order at an eatery, when you are sunbathing and when you visit the loo. Yes, even the loo, because time is precious and you want to make the most of whatever little time you have. As for most women, the washroom is the only place where she has undisturbed time for herself. That's why I suggested this list of activities that earn us some free time to put LOA into practice.

My all-time favourite hobby is affirmation. I keep doing it perpetually every time I get the opportunity. I also affirm in the singing mode because singing makes me happy and heightens my vibration. Affirmation appeared tough for me too in the initial stages as I was in a mental turmoil struggling to convince myself to accept what I was repeatedly chanting.

For example, I had gained weight and put on 12 kilos after an accident. I outgrew most of my clothes and was desperate to get back to shape and go back to my previous weight. I began affirming that I am slim … Nothing happened for a month because I was finding it troublesome to believe that I am slim as I could see myself bloating from all sides. I avoided the mirror but it didn't help in the least. Besides, it was a struggle every single day, managing to squeeze into my clothes and even worse trying to get out of them without the stitches of my existing outfit falling apart.

15

I looked even scarier without my clothes on! From 48 kilos I had moved to 65 kilos. In my eyes, I was fat. I looked disastrous in almost all the outfits I wore and imagine my plight every time I told myself "I am slim." This sentence wasn't sinking into my mind no matter how much I tried saying it to myself. Somewhere within me, I was unable to accept it. I could not fake it to my own self. Then I began seeing my old albums and pictures where I was indeed slim. That's when I realized I could go back to my earlier weight, as I was slim at some point of time in my life. Only when this aspect of my thought process sunk in my being, my affirmations made sense and I started seeing changes.

Likewise, you could begin by first affirming *what is believable* for you and then switch on to other aspects or areas that have not yet materialised. In this way, it becomes far easier to affirm anything at all or else, you would create a mental block without realizing it. This appears to be the hurdle and you fail in your capability to manifest and finally conclude that the affirmations don't work for you.

Affirming means you are acknowledging certain information and chanting repetitive sentences to influence your subconscious mind to enable the process of manifestation. The expression used in affirmations is the language of *feeling* that you convey in the sentence. Otherwise, words are basically hollow and mean very little.

You need to feel the words when you say something like "I am financially abundant." The feeling here is the energy that you put forth which is an absolute necessity.

Ensure you are speaking *in the present* tense. Affirmations have to be in the present tense. Rather than saying "I will be…" or "I am going to be…" or "I see myself as someone who is going to be…," you can frame your sentences more effectively. Every sentence above implies that it is going to happen, but not immediately or soon enough. It may likely happen but in the future. You must be certain your affirmations indicate that it is happening in the now, in the present moment. Rather than saying "I will…," you could preferably choose to emphasize "I am…"

Let me quote another example, "I will be successful" is an incorrect affirmation if you are aiming to be successful soon enough.

Instead, how about adopting, "I am successful." This is a rather correct affirmation.

Affirmations must necessarily consist of *positive words or sentences*. The Universe does not understand negative words like 'don't' or 'won't' or 'can't' and many more. Hence, avoid using them in your statements.

For example, "I don't want my boss to yell at me today." This sentence is incorrectly phrased and if you affirm the above, you are likely to bring forth what you affirm but, as the Universe cannot understand the word 'don't,' the sentence implies, "I want my boss to yell at me today." Instead, you could write the same sentence in a positive manner: "My boss appreciates me today" or "My boss is full of praises for my work today."

Learn to frame simple sentences that are easy to recite and recall.

Affirmations have a better impact if you follow the *mirror effect*. If you affirm looking into the mirror, it becomes more effective. The affirmation tends to be more productive for you. Affirm while meeting your eyes in the mirror. It is like looking into your soul when you have eye contact with yourself in the mirror. The effect is phenomenal.

Lastly, you need to be very *specific* while affirming. When you say "I am abundant," it does not suffice. You have to specify what exactly you are in abundance of: "I am financially abundant." You need to be as specific and precise as possible.

I am convinced about the impact of affirmation in my life,

especially if it's applied accurately. Continuous affirmations have gotten me so many things at the drop of a hat.

b) *Visualisation with a vision board*

Visualisation is my weakness. I love doing it. I am addicted to this method of the Law of Attraction because it works for me every single time.

In the last couple of years, I have numerous manifestations to cite but I would like to share one of my first manifestations here the credit of which goes to applying the method of visualisation. I wanted to have six months' vacation in London and therefore, had stacked away a small sum of money in the bank in the form of fixed deposits. I had taken a break from my high-paying job and was helping out in a small-time startup with a friend who couldn't pay me much, but it did give me a great deal of leisure time. I was cautious when it came to dealing with my finances as I planned to take the six months' vacation in London soon and needed the money for the same.

After reading extensively on the LOA and being an extremely positive person, I decided to apply the visualisation method to the best of my effort.

One article in a magazine, featuring London in all its glory, had me yearning to be there as soon as possible. I promptly made a vision board and put up amazing pictures of eateries, cuisines, must-visit historical places, business class journeys and pictures of the arrival area inside the airport and another picture clearly showing 'Welcome to Heathrow.'

My vision board specifically indicated that I wanted my journey too to be as enriching as my stay in London. I started working with my gratitude list, affirmations and visualisations. I refused to be bogged down by any contradicting suggestions from my friends who spotted my vision board. Their recommendations for me to visit New Zealand instead, as the government was more open to Indians visiting the country, fell on deaf ears. I stood my ground. Nothing was going to deter me from having my vacation of six months in London.

I believed with every fibre in my heart that I was already in London. I visualised visiting Madame Tussauds museum and taking pictures with my favourite film personalities. I visualised meeting and hanging out with some of my friends settled in London. I was having fun and drinks and partying with them in my imagination. Nothing could prevent me from chasing this desire. I had made up my mind to live in London.

I planned to visit London in October as I wished to experience the enchanting sight of snowflakes. I had never seen snow in my entire life.

I live in India and cotton summer clothes are preferable with the climate being unbearably hot. I broke one of my small savings and went winter shopping, signalling to the Universe that I was getting ready to travel. I neither had the kind of money to stay in London for six months nor did I have any idea about the visa formalities. Yet I was contemplating on how to go about it.

Luckily for me, as fate would have it, one of my cousins needed to travel to London to buy some machinery and he asked me out of the blue if I would like to join him. I was stunned for several moments on the phone before I gladly responded that it was my dream to visit London. It appeared like the Universe was working full-time solely for me. My cousin had only one condition. I would be carrying two small machines on my return and he would be carrying the other two which needed urgent repair. I agreed readily. I was on cloud nine.

Of all the places in this world, what are the chances my cousin would ask me to join him to London? But he did. The minute I said "Yes" to London, I knew in my heart and soul that I was going to London, come what may!

I was happy and thrilled. With this positive frame of mind, I got my visa effortlessly despite barely having any bank balance in my account. I did not even have a credit card, yet the Universe worked it out for me. The ticket was sponsored by my cousin and it was Indian Rs. 270 from India to London. Everything was magically unfolding for me. My local travel within India cost far more than the unbelievably measly Rs. 270. My return ticket from London to India was Rs. 10,000. Overall, it was incredible.

I went on a fully sponsored trip with my cousin. My visualisation worked to the extent that I was upgraded along with him to business class as he was a frequent traveller and I stayed for nearly six months in London with some additional cash gifted to me by my mom. I visited most of the historical museums, held hands with my favourite actors Shahrukh, Aishwarya and Amitabh at Madame Tussauds, touched the snowflakes and tasted several spoonfuls of snow!

I had also asked for a special gift from the Universe,

something that was uncommon. Something I had never experienced before. I was gifted a blue rose by a friend. I had never seen a blue rose before in my life. So imagine how special I felt looking at one. I must have clicked a hundred pictures of the blue rose and sent it to all my friends in India.

The most astonishing part was that I was upgraded to business class on my solo return from London to India. I must admit that everything was dreamlike and it is still one of my most cherished memories. Life is indeed amazing!

Visualisation is the key... Every single thing on my vision board materialised. Even though I lacked the resources, money or knowledge, I still visited and stayed in London for six months! I had only immense faith that I would be in London and the Universe paved the path for me.

Don't contradict your visualisation with negative statements or thoughts. Don't doubt it. Keep your focus on the end result and things will work out automatically for you.

I am a living example that anything and everything is possible if you set your mind to it. Remain focused and have a burning desire to see yourself experiencing your desires not just in dreams but in reality too.

c) *The water magic*

60% of our body consists of water and water has the immense ability to affect us. So whatever thoughts you put into water manifests into reality accordingly. This has been proved by the experiments done by Dr. Masaru Emoto.

To do this activity that I do, you need to have four things. A bottle of water, a pen, a piece of paper and your faith! Take a glass bottle or a copper glass filled with water that you can consume all day long or just for this purpose. Write down what you desire on the piece of paper. Keep the pen aside.

Take the paper and keep it on the ground or on a table in front of you. Keep the water on top of the paper. You can start by tapping your forehead between your eyebrows with your forefinger and middle finger for a few seconds. It is done to awaken your Third Eye chakra. Next, you can place your palms together as if in a prayer position and begin to rub it against each other vigorously, all along visualising your desires. You can close your eyes and do it. When you cannot rub your palms against each other anymore, stop. Palm the cup with both your hands. Let the energy move from your palms to the water. Don't lift or move the glass or mug. Continue visualising your desires until you are quite done. You can do it for three to five minutes. Then start drinking the water in the glass or mug.

Whatever you visualised or put your energy into achieving, is most likely to materialise as that is what you are consuming into yourself. The sentence must be in the now and absolutely positive. Words like 'don't,' 'can't,' 'will,' 'need' must be avoided at all costs.

Alternatively, some of you can also wrap the paper, with your wish written on it, around the bottle or glass with your energised palms, before you begin to visualise for three to five minutes. If it's a one-liner statement, you can also paste it on the glass itself. If you cannot visualise, you can affirm the written desire, mentally or aloud. You can also just be grateful for everything you already have. Gratitude will get you more reasons to be grateful. The positive energy will help you manifest your wishes into reality in the most miraculous manner.

You can keep the paper stuck on the glass if you plan to repeat the process or you can practise it until your desire is fulfilled, in case you have put in a date to manifest. You can discard the paper when the wish is manifested.

It is a very effective practice. Do follow it religiously for a couple of weeks, concentrating on any one thing in your life and see for yourself the wonders that happen in your life.

d) Cup to cup method

Take two glasses. Paste your current life situation on one cup and what you desire onto the next cup. Pour drinking water into the current cup.

Now, the current cup with water signifies your current situation in life.

For example, you are a single guy who is lonely and unhappy, you are yearning for a partner in your life, you want someone to date, you want someone to spend time with and you want to enjoy life's romantic moments with your significant other and much more. Admit whatever your current situation is. Although the paper pasted on the glass might state a one-liner that "I am single and lonely," you might make more statements when you hold the cup. You can say anything and everything about your current situation in life. You can even admit that you are sad or just voice out facts like "I make $5000 a month" or whatever your current situation is.

Pour the water from the cup signifying your current life, to the cup denoting your desired life. The sentence pasted on the desire cup could be "I desire to have an amazing partner in my life as soon as possible" or whatever you are seeking. You can repeat the line or add any more sentences you wish verbally. Then you can drink the water from the desired cup.

This is quantum jumping. It takes you from where you are to where you desire to be. A small tuning in your belief and you are exactly where you want to be!

This never fails me. So I recommend you too could try it, for sure.

4. THE NIGHT ROUTINE

Every routine has a role to play when it comes to manifesting your dreams. The routine you follow every night plays a vital role. It is significant as to what you think of or hear about or listen to or read about just before you sleep off in the night. That is important because the last activity you do just before you sleep extends into your subconscious mind and remains there for a much longer period than when you are intentionally doing it.

So these thoughts claim your subconscious mind all through your sleep period and that's far more time than you can ever do it when you are awake, with a conscious effort. Therefore, it's very important to have the right frame of mind, comprising of a sense of state of absolute calmness that is completely free from stress, before you hit the bed, in order to attract what you want in life.

You need to calm your mind before you sleep. There are roughly about 70,000 thoughts per day, and we are conscious of only about 5% of our cognitive activity. Most of our action, behaviour, and emotions depend on 95% of our brain activity that goes beyond our conscious awareness.

Calm your mind by breathing deeply… Get off social media or television, and quit watching horror or action movies because you are attracting the problems and issues occurring in the lives of others into your life as your own. Hence, refrain from doing it well about a couple of hours prior to hitting the bed.

Many of you might state that you are busy, often running out of time, you need to check your mails frequently as there are important messages, Facebook messages, LinkedIn or any other social sites, just before you hit the bed. If you want your desires to manifest, you need to make some effort and sacrifices. Keep your addictions at bay.

Put in a bit of effort and you get quick results … or keep doing what you want and struggle throughout your life. What do you prefer?

Obviously, the easier way out!

Emotion is energy, so what happens is that when you invest your feelings and energy into anything that you are keen to attract, it simply creates magic back in return by bringing your desire into reality.

Feelings tend to have the ability to speed up your manifestation. Mere thoughts will be futile but where there is an attachment of thoughts to emotions, the manifestation process will amaze you.

29

Thus emotion or feeling is the key to this puzzle of manifestation.

If you follow the methods mentioned above, you are intentionally setting yourself up for success. You are going to achieve all your dreams and make it a reality. You are going to be a role model for many others around you. You will become the inspiration for everyone who knows you. Each of these methods has been a boon when it came to manifesting anything I have ever desired.

The Law of Attraction works like a magic wand in my life. I have attracted money out of nowhere, travelled to some of my dream destinations, and stayed for nearly a month in the best of hotels. I can afford to wear the most exquisite designer wears that I have always dreamt of. Being a foodie, I also have had the opportunity of sampling and savouring cuisines from different countries in the world. My life is truly dreamlike and I am madly in love with my life and everyone around me. I look much younger than my age and I consider myself blessed to the core. All thanks to this insightful knowledge that has helped me immensely.

Being a millionaire, having your dream house, holidaying in the best of countries, or wearing the dream outfit that you wish, will no longer be an unfulfilled wish. Scratch it off your wish list. Nothing can be more real than your ability to bring it into experience. Keep your belief and faith intact and everything is a possibility.

I have realized that I am the genie of my life and I have the power to use the magic wand in my life the way I want! I urge everyone who reads this book to discover it in your own way!

Be blessed!

www.ingramcontent.com/pod-product-compliance
Lightning Source LLC
Chambersburg PA
CBHW020445030426
42337CB00014B/1407